# Behind the Scenes

## at the Airport

by **Marilyn Miller**
illustrated by **Ingo Fast**

RSVP

RAINTREE
STECK-VAUGHN
PUBLISHERS
The Steck-Vaughn Company

*Austin, Texas*

Published by Raintree Steck-Vaughn Publishers,
an imprint of Steck-Vaughn Company
Developed for Steck-Vaughn Company by
Visual Education Corporation, Princeton, New Jersey
Project Director: Paula McGuire
Production Supervision: Barbara A. Kopel
Electronic Preparation: Cynthia C. Feldner
Art Director: Maxson Crandall

**Raintree Steck-Vaughn Publishers**
Editor: Pamela Wells
Project Manager: Joyce Spicer


**Library of Congress Cataloging-in-Publication Data**
Miller, Marilyn F.
Behind the scenes at the airport / Marilyn F. Miller : illustrated by Ingo Fast.
p.    cm. —
Includes bibliographical references and index.
Summary: Looks behind the scenes of an airport at how everything works
including the ticket counter, the control room, and the flight kitchen.
ISBN 0-8172-4086-1
1. Airports—Juvenile literature.  [1. Airports.]  I. Fast, Ingo, ill.   II. Title.
TL725.15.M54    1996
387.7´36—dc20    95-19603    CIP    AC


Printed and bound in the United States
1 2 3 4 5 6 7 8 9 0  IP  99 98 97 96 95

# Table of Contents

**C**ome visit behind the scenes of an airport. Look inside and see how everything works.

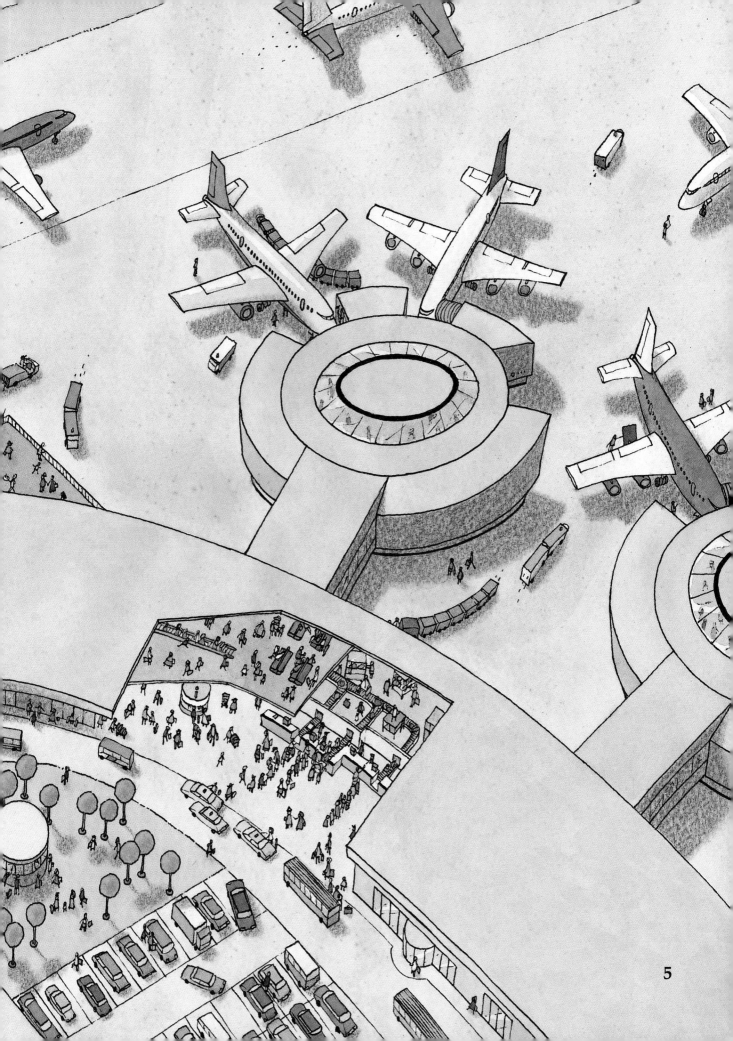

# Getting Around

Buses, cars, taxis, and vans take people to and from the airport. Special roads allow people to be let off at the airport terminal entrances. The terminal is the main airport building for passengers.

Do you see the parking areas near the terminal? People can park their cars there. See the trucks. They bring goods to the airport. Find the cargo building. Goods are stored here.

Here are cars on the highway to the airport. Signs show drivers the way to the right terminal, or building.

# Ticket to Ride

Every airline has a ticket counter in the passenger terminal. Here, passengers decide where to sit. They may choose the rear, middle, or front of the plane. They also choose a window or an aisle seat.

8

Do you see the passengers leaving the ticket counter? They are going to the gate, or entrance, leading to their plane. The passengers are carrying small bags and special passes. These passes allow them to enter, or board, the plane.

Ticket counter workers use computers to print tickets quickly. Computers are also used to check for any empty seats on a flight. Most large airplanes can carry up to 250 passengers. A 747 jet seats 412 passengers.

Here is a passenger going through a special machine that would show a weapon, like a gun or a knife. All passengers must pass through it.

9

# Bags and Baggage

A truck brings bags and suitcases from the plane to the baggage area. There they are put on a moving circular platform.

Do you see the passengers looking for their suitcases? Passengers use special tickets called claims checks to pick up their baggage. Workers make sure passengers take the right suitcases.

Below, a passenger shows his passport. A passport tells the person's name, date of birth, and country. It also has his or her picture. Special workers check the passports of all people arriving on flights from other countries.

Pets travel in a special section of the plane. A tag on the pet's crate shows where the pet is going and any special care it needs.

# Ready for the Next Trip

Passengers leave the plane from the front. At the same time, workers who clean the plane enter from the rear. That way the plane will be ready for the next flight.

Do you see the worker putting a magazine in the pocket of the seat? Workers clean headsets, vacuum floors, and clean the bathrooms, too.

At airports where planes from other countries land, all trash from every flight is burned. That way people are protected from diseases that may have been carried into the United States.

Here is a cleaner with full trash bags. The bags contain old newspapers, magazines, and trash.

# Feeding the Passengers

An airline worker called the dietician uses the computer to plan meals. The computer helps the dietician see how much food and drink is needed for each flight.

Here is a flight attendant carrying a food tray for the meal wagon.

Some airlines have their own flight kitchens at the airport. There, food for each flight is prepared. Other airlines buy their meals from a company that prepares the food.

Food, juices, and soft drinks arrive on a truck. They are stored in the plane's kitchen, or galley. Do you see the flight attendants with the meal cart in the rear section? They are about to serve the passengers.

Some passengers may ask for special food. Special meals may have only a little salt or no meat. Most airlines make a note of special meals for passengers when they buy tickets. The special meals are kept in the galley.

Find the girl who is looking for the meal cart.

# Fueling the Plane

The aircraft is filled with fuel in its parking area before each flight. Mechanics fuel the plane from underneath using large trucks called tankers.

Do you see the worker reading the meter? A 747 jet can carry over 47,000 gallons (178,000 liters) of fuel. It can fly more than 6,000 miles (9,700 kilometers) without needing more fuel. It takes about ten minutes to put fuel into a passenger jet.

Here, a worker is reading a tag. He wants to make sure the suitcase is going on the cart for the correct plane.

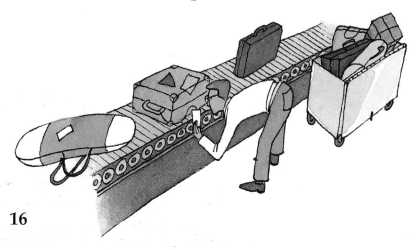

Here comes the fire truck.
Firefighters always stand by
during fueling in case
of fire.

# Tending the Fleet

Some people work on an aircraft when it is not flying. They are called the ground crew. They check the plane to make sure it is working right. Mechanics test engines and other parts. They make small repairs when the plane is parked near the terminal. Spare parts are kept in a storage room, or stockroom.

Here is a plane entering a hangar.
Hangars are parking garages
for aircraft. Mechanics
can make big repairs
when aircraft are in hangars.

All planes must have a
complete checkup after they fly a certain
number of hours. This checkup takes about
a week. The airline does small checks more often.
A 747's tires are changed about 48 times a year.

# While You Wait

People wait in the passenger terminal for flights to arrive and depart. Passengers and their friends may sit in special waiting areas before a flight. Do you see a passenger in the news store? The terminal has many stores and places to eat. It also has bank machines and, sometimes, even a post office.

Sometimes passengers who are waiting need help. Most airports have a special agency to help travelers with problems. The airlines also give wheelchairs to people who need them to get around.

A terminal for flights in and out of the country has a duty-free shop. This duty-free shop allows people to buy things without paying special taxes on them.

# The Tower

Some workers guide takeoffs and landings. These air traffic controllers work in the control tower. They also direct planes that are moving on the ground. Some airports have the tower on top of the terminal.

Traffic controllers use the radio to give instructions to pilots. Do you see the controllers looking out the windows? These giant windows give a clear view of the whole airport.

Here are other controllers in the radar room below the tower. They are using radio signals to find distant objects. Screens show how fast and high each plane near the airport is flying. Radar guides aircraft when bad weather makes seeing difficult.

Controllers at big airports direct about 200 takeoffs and 200 landings every hour. A 747 jet's landing speed is about 200 miles per hour. Some runways for big planes are as long as 14,000 feet (4,300 meters). Smaller planes can use shorter runways.

Find the person who is climbing up into the tower.

# Keeping People Informed

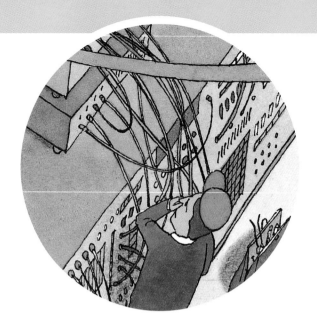

The terminal's control room has all the newest information about flights to and from the airport. Do you see the main computer? Information is fed into it by each airline's computers. The airline reports when a flight will take off that day. It also reports when the plane will land.

Sometimes a flight may leave early or late. A plane may have a new landing time, too.

The weather may also be bad. Then, the airline may give the control room a new time for a plane's takeoff or landing.

Here is a woman looking at a computer screen, or monitor. It shows each flight's landing, or arrival, time. The monitor is run by the control room. Monitors are found in many places in the passenger terminal. In this way people can have the newest flight information.

# Captains of the Sky

The flight crew flies the aircraft from the cockpit. There are many controls in front of the captain. The captain and co-captain are in charge of them.

Do you see the flight engineer checking the dials? They show information about the engine, such as how much fuel is left. The plane's speed, how high it is, and where it is all show on the screen. This information helps keep the plane on the correct course, or direction.

Here are the captain and co-captain during the flight. Sometimes the weather is so bad that they cannot see ahead. Then a machine called an autopilot keeps the plane on the correct course.

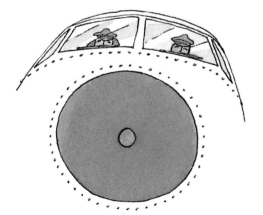

A pilot must have 1,500 hours of flying before becoming the captain of a passenger plane.

Find the window in the cockpit.

# Lift Off!

Many small airports have one runway. Large airports have several runways. How does a plane reach the runway from its parking spot? It taxis, or moves slowly on the ground, over a short strip of concrete that leads to the runway.

Do you see the plane taking off? The speed of a 727 jet at takeoff is about 140 miles per hour.

Here is a ground worker using hand signals. He is guiding the plane from its parking spot to the runway. Ground workers may use flashlights at night.

The pilot waits at the start of the runway for the control tower to tell him or her to taxi. Big white numbers painted at each end of the runway help guide pilots. At night, lights make the runways easy to see.

29

# Glossary

The **baggage area** is where passengers pick up their bags and suitcases after a flight.

The **cockpit** is where the flight crew flies the plane from.

The **control room** has all the latest information about flights to and from the airport.

The **duty-free shop** is where people buy items without paying a special tax on them.

The **flight kitchen** is where an airline prepares its food for each flight. Some airlines have their own flight kitchens at the airport.

The **galley** is the plane's kitchen.

The **hangar** is a building where planes are parked. Mechanics make big repairs there.

The **parking area** is where the plane is fueled for the next flight.

The **runway** is where planes take off from and land.

The **terminal** is the main airport building serving passengers.

The **ticket counter** is where passengers buy tickets for flights.

The **tower** is where air traffic controllers guide takeoffs and landings.

# Further Readings

*Aircraft: An Educational Coloring Book.* Spizzirri, Linda (ed.). Rapid City, South Dakota: Spizzirri, 1981.

Asimov, Isaac. *How Do Airplanes Fly?* Milwaukee: Gareth Stevens, Inc., 1992.

Bauer, Judith. *What It's Like to Be an Airline Pilot.* Mahwah, New Jersey: Troll Associates, 1990.

Magee, Doug, and Newman, Robert. *Let's Fly from A to Z.* New York: Dutton, 1992.

# Index